Crabapples

A Canoe Trip

Bobbie Kalman

Crabtree Publishing Company

Crabapples

created by Bobbie Kalman

for Peter and Samantha, a couple of avid canoe trippers

Editor-in-Chief
Bobbie Kalman

Writers/editors
Bobbie Kalman
Tammy Everts
David Schimpky
Samantha Crabtree

Managing editor
Lynda Hale

Computer design
Lynda Hale
David Schimpky

Color separations and film
Dot 'n Line Image Inc.

Printer
Worzalla Publishing Company

Illustrations
Barb Bedell
Ellen O'Hara: page 27

Special thanks to
Steven Hemming at YMCA Camp Wanakita; Jocelyn Palm at Glen Bernard Camp; Joyce Schimpky at Camp Crossroads; the children from YMCA Camp Wanakita who appear in this book: Ryan Burton, Malcolm Dalgliesh, Julian Dalgliesh, Jan Drewniak, James Fraser, Chris Merrick, Milos Milojevic, Daniel Minnick, Amy Wheeler, Emil Wijnker, Mark Wijnker, and Paul Wilton

Photographs
All photographs by Marc Crabtree, except the following:

Camp Crossroads: pages 22-23
Glen Bernard Camp: page 24 (bottom)
Heather Halfyard: pages 13 (right), 25 (right)
Industry, Science, and Technology (ISTC): pages 20, 27 (both)
Don Standfield: pages 7 (top), 9, 14 (bottom), 15 (top)

Every attempt has been made to secure model releases for the pictures used in this book.

Crabtree Publishing Company

350 Fifth Avenue
Suite 3308
New York
N.Y. 10118

360 York Road, RR 4,
Niagara-on-the-Lake,
Ontario, Canada
L0S 1J0

73 Lime Walk
Headington
Oxford OX3 7AD
United Kingdom

Cataloging in Publication Data

Kalman, Bobbie, 1947-
   A canoe trip

(Crabapples)
Includes index
ISBN 0-86505-619-6 (library bound) ISBN 0-86505-719-2 (pbk.)
This book shows the many parts of a canoe trip, including packing, paddling skills, camping, and safety.

1. Canoes and canoeing - Juvenile literature. 2. Camping - Juvenile literature. I. Title. II. Series: Kalman, Bobbie, 1947- Crabapples.

GV 789.K35 1995   j 797.1'22   LC 94-44937
                                                                                CIP

What is in this book?

A canoe trip

Canoes have been around for thousands of years. The Native peoples of North America used light, sturdy canoes made of birch bark to travel across lakes and along rivers and streams.

Today, we use canoes mostly for fun. At many summer camps, one of the activities is a canoe trip in the wilderness.

Join us on a camp canoe trip. Paddle beside thick forests and rolling hills. Enjoy a delicious lunch cooked over an open fire. Take a refreshing break and leap into a cold lake. Brrr! Find new ways to explore the wonders of nature!

Parts of a canoe

Canoes still look the same as they did hundreds of years ago. Although many canoes are now made of modern materials, some are still made of wood.

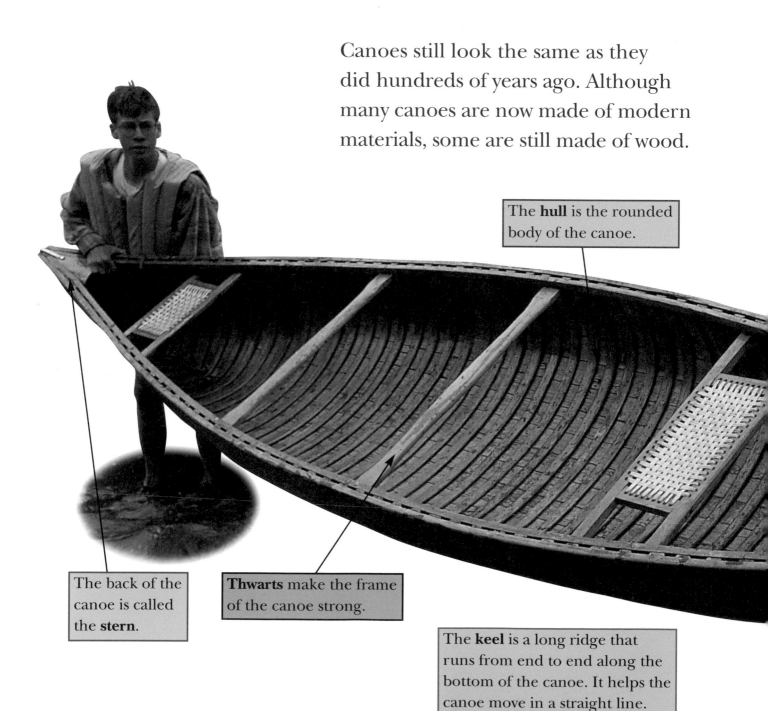

The **hull** is the rounded body of the canoe.

The back of the canoe is called the **stern**.

Thwarts make the frame of the canoe strong.

The **keel** is a long ridge that runs from end to end along the bottom of the canoe. It helps the canoe move in a straight line.

Canoes can be big or small. Very large canoes can carry over 20 people. Two people sit side by side on each seat.

The canoe below is built to carry one, two, or three people. Two people can sit on the seats, and a passenger can ride in the middle.

The **gunnels** are the upper edges of the canoe's sides.

The front of the canoe is called the **bow**.

Using a paddle

Paddling a canoe on calm water is easy. You stretch your arms forward and pull your paddle through the water in a long, straight stroke. The person paddling in the bow sets the pace for everyone else in the canoe.

The person paddling in the stern has the hardest job. He or she has to steer the canoe with special strokes. One steering stroke is called the **J-stroke**. If you look at this drawing, you can see why it is called a J-stroke.

Ready to go

What to bring

✓ – bug spray and sunscreen
✓ – hat
✓ – rain coat
✓ – hiking shoes or boots
✓ – swim suit and towel
✓ – soap, toothbrush, and toothpaste
✓ – toilet paper
✓ – flashlight
✓ – sleeping bag
✓ – ground cloth for putting under
    sleeping bag
✓ – a change of clothes

You are about to begin a week-long canoe trip. The camp counselors have planned the trip carefully. They have made a list of what each person should bring. By sharing things like tents, food, mess kits, and soap, each camper can pack a lot less.

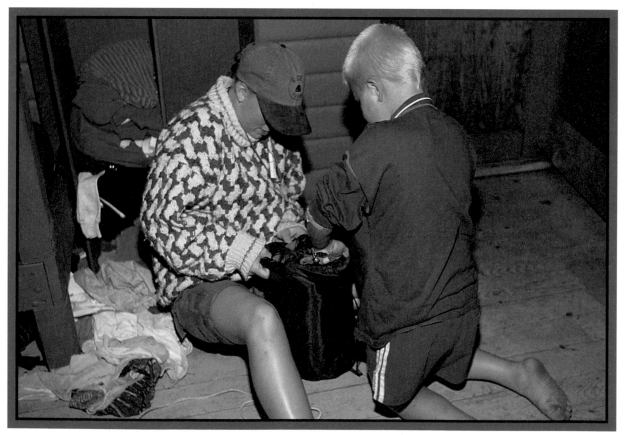

Your counselors have met with the camp director to plan your route and decide how long your trip will last. This information will help the camp find you in case of an emergency.

Canoe safety

Before you begin your trip, you must learn about canoe safety. With one mistake, you could end up in the water before you even leave the shore!

Make sure that you always wear a life jacket when you are on the water. Your life jacket should fit properly. It must be completely fastened so it won't come off.

To get into the canoe, place your paddle across the gunnels for support. Lean against the paddle as you step into the canoe, and then sit down.

Do not stand up in the canoe unless you are getting in or out. You might fall into the water or tip the canoe over. Your things will get soaked!

Paddle close to shore in case the canoe tips. A tipped canoe will still float. Hold on to the canoe and kick your feet. When you get to land, you can dry off.

Portage!

You are traveling down a narrow river when you hear the sound of rushing water. As you round a bend in the river, you realize that you are approaching a waterfall! You paddle to the shore, but you still have to get past the waterfall. What do you do? You **portage**!

Portaging means carrying boats and supplies over land. It can be very difficult if your pack is heavy. Sometimes you have to cross mucky swamps. Ugh! LEECHES!

Portaging is a welcome rest from paddling. You can enjoy a snack and look for wildlife. When your portage is done, plop your canoe in the water and start paddling again!

Pitching camp

After a long day of canoeing, it is time to pitch camp and relax. Many parks have sites ready for camping, but sometimes campers have to create their own campsite.

Look for a flat area that does not have puddles. Clear the stones, sticks, and pine cones from the area where you want to set up the tents. A pebble will feel like a boulder if you have to lie on it all night!

16

Don't forget to dig a toilet! Make sure that the hole is well away from the shore. The toilet should be about a foot deep. Do not put your toilet paper in the hole. Instead, burn it in the fire. Fill in the hole when you leave the campsite.

Next, choose a spot for a fire pit. It must not be close to trees, dry grass, or anything that might catch fire easily. Dig a shallow hole and place rocks around it. Gather twigs and birch bark to start your fire.

Camp safety

There are some important safety rules you need to remember when you are at the campsite.

If you go swimming, do not dive into the water until you have made sure that the water is deep enough. You can be badly injured if you dive into shallow water.

Beware of poisonous plants! Some berries may look delicious, but do not eat them unless an adult is sure they are safe. When walking in a forest, wear long pants or pull your socks up high. If your skin touches poison ivy, poison sumac, or poison oak, you can get a very itchy rash!

Flames can spread quickly, so someone should always watch the campfire. Make sure the fire is out when you go to bed or leave the campsite! Pour several buckets of water on the fire pit.

poison ivy

poison oak

poison sumac

Bear trouble

If a bear visits your camp, it wants your food, not you. You can do a few simple things to "bear-proof" your camp.

Smells attract bears, so wash your dishes right after eating. Do not keep food, or even toothpaste, in your tent.

Tie a strong piece of rope to the pack containing the food. Throw the free end over a sturdy branch. Hoist the bag as high as possible and tie the end of the rope securely to the trunk of the tree.

Chow time!

There is nothing like dinner cooked outdoors. You cannot make pizza or french fries, but the bannock recipe on the opposite page tastes great cooked over a campfire!

Here is a list of some groceries for your canoe trip:

Food list
- pancake mix
- maple syrup
- breakfast cereal
- powdered milk
- sugar
- macaroni and cheese mix
- dried soup mix
- beef jerky
- bannock mix
- eggs (use on the first day)
- dried fruit
- raisins and nuts

Bannock

Bannock is a traditional camping bread. Before you leave for your trip, mix 2 cups (500 ml) of flour, a tablespoon (15 ml) of baking powder, a tablespoon of sugar, some raisins, and a pinch of salt together in a strong freezer bag.

Mix the dry ingredients with 2 cups of water, an egg, and a bit of vegetable oil. This recipe makes three dough patties. Double it to get more! Wrap each patty around the end of a thick, clean stick. Turn the bannock over the fire until it is cooked evenly. Let it cool and then share and enjoy!

Drinking water

It is important to have good, clean water when you are camping. You need water for cooking and drinking.

Sometimes river or lake water carries germs that can make you very sick. To kill the germs, you can boil the water. The simplest and best way to clean water is to use a portable water filter. You can buy a water filter at a camping-goods store.

Respecting the environment

When you leave your campsite, make it look as though you had never been there. The next visitors to the campsite do not want to clean up your mess!

Garbage must be burned or "packed out" of the park in a garbage bag. Do not burn plastic, styrofoam, or metal.

Biodegradable soap is less harmful to the earth than other kinds of soap. Dump your dirty water far away from the lake.

Only dead or fallen wood should be burned in the campfire. Tearing bark from a live tree can kill the tree.

Enjoying nature

What is your reward for respecting nature? As you paddle across a lake or hike through a forest, look at the world around you. You may see a playful raccoon, a hawk soaring in the sky, or maybe even a baby deer!

You can admire the beauty of the flowers and the majesty of the mighty trees. Listen to the calling of birds and the chirping of insects. Take a deep breath of fresh air. The wonders of nature make the extra work of earth-friendly camping worthwhile.

Lost in the woods

In the evening, you decide to go for a walk in the woods. You hear the sound of rushing water and run toward it to investigate. After walking for a few minutes, you find a beautiful waterfall.

You want to tell your friends, so you start heading back to the campsite—but which way should you go? All the trees look the same. You are lost!

There are some things you can do to avoid getting lost. Do not wander away from the campsite by yourself. If you go exploring with a friend, make sure you stay on the trails.

If you do get lost, stay where you are. Someone will find you soon. If you keep walking, you could end up even more confused! Carry a whistle on a string around your neck so you can blow it to help searchers find you. Don't worry— soon you will be back with your friends!

Trip scrapbook

mallard duck

When your canoe trip is over, you will have plenty of great memories. Perhaps you will remember a beautiful starry night, singing around the campfire, or seeing a moose. Experiences that did not seem funny at the time will seem very funny when you think about them later. Remember the rainstorm that filled the canoe with water? Will you ever forget the leeches in your breeches?

moose

You can keep memories of your canoe trip in many ways. Making a scrapbook is a great way to remember your trip. You can write funny stories, jokes, rhymes, and helpful tips for your next trip. Make sketches of the animals you saw. If you have a camera, take photos and tape them in your scrapbook.

Words to know

biodegradable soap Soap that is less harmful to the environment than other kinds of soap

environment The area in which plants, animals, and people live

gunnel The upper edge of a canoe's sides

leech A worm that lives in water and sucks blood from animals

mess kit A small kit of pans, dishes, and cutlery

portage To carry boats and supplies from one waterway to another

styrofoam A kind of light plastic used to make disposable cups

thwart A wooden beam that makes a canoe's hull strong

Index

1 2 3 4 5 6 7 8 9 0 Printed in USA 4 3 2 1 0 9 8 7 6 5